Christian Poems and Other Radical Explorations

To
miss
Stephaine
God bless you.
Hope it is a blessing
to you!

[illegible]

5/26

Christian Poems and Other Radical Explorations

Poet Ntwadumela

Heart of David

III

Published by Heart of David

Published in the United States of America

ISBN-978-1475221268

First Heart of David Printing 2012

Dedicated to Dorothy M. Harper (Ma)

You always understood
and knew the reasons why.

Poet Ntwadumela online

poetntw.com
Poet Ntwadumela on facebook
poetntwadumela on twitter
vrblntwadumela on twitter
wordntwadumela on twitter

Chapbooks
From the Valley of Elah
From Mount Carmel

CONTENTS

I Poems

II Other Radical Explorations

Introduction

This book of poetry is simply a humble attempt to answer God's call as stated in "Parable" the last piece in this work. Poetry is important to any society and the poet has an important responsibility. The poet must show us ourselves and the world around us without compromise, failing this he or she ceases to be a poet and becomes something less than true. The poet must encourage, accuse, reveal, and represent the society around him or her without regard to how that society might receive the given views and observations. Any society that does not value objective observation about itself is a society in danger of becoming the worst that it can be. Few others can stand within a society but speak to it as an outsider as the poet can and must.

The Christian poet's responsibility is greater still for he or she must stay true to the spirit of God beyond their own passions and expectations. The Christian poet must speak a message to all people that at times is as difficult to speak as it is to hear. Therefore God's poet must be an intercessor, representing God to people and even people to God to bring reconciliation and healing. One need only look at the psalms of David to understand the scope of the human plea spoken by such a poet. One can also look at the prophet Jeremiah to see how the poet can speak for God to a society in need of change. By using these two examples I am not saying that all poets are prophets but it is not a stretch to presume that all prophets are poets.

This shouldn't be a surprise to us for we are told in Ephesians 2:10 that God himself is the master Poet. The word rendered workmanship in English in that scripture is in the original Greek poiema. Poiema is where we get our English word poem. We our God's crafted expression. We are God's poem.

It is in this spirit that I submit these few poems to be a help and ministry to those who find them useful. It is my hope that you would read through these various pages and be blessed.

Poet Ntwadumela 2012

P.S. Ntwadumela (In-twy-do-may-la) means, "He Who Greets With Fire." With the various biblical examples of God in the old and new testiments manifesting his presence as fire, Poet Ntwadumela simply means the poet who greets with the presence of God.

And David said, “What have I done now? Is there not a cause?” 1Sam17:29 NKJV

I

CHRISTIAN POEMS

Autumn Tears (Gal 3:13)

Tree weeps blood red leaves.
Recalling perhaps tree cursed
sin hung blood drop red.

Labels and Questions

Christian has come to mean
something other than "Little Christ."

Some things like "judge, jury, executioner."
or "Very nice and very fake."

We are perceived as the culture
and its master intends.

Do we work hard enough to
topple this stacked deck?

Or do we plant it, water it,
contribute to its growth?

Christians must live in this world submerged,
this world baptized in Noah's flood.

The questions: "Keep on your helmet?"
or "Tragically inhale the water?"

In any case there is God up above in the light
lovingly working the pumps.

The Double Life Chant

The double life
Is the wicked life
Plus the cover life
This is the double life
The cover life
Hides the wicked life
And the wicked life
Grows on.

The wicked life
Halts the Godly life
And the Godly life
Holds the future life
And the future life
Guards the soul life
From decaying in
The world.

The cankerworm
And the palmerworm
Assault the soul life
Through the wicked life
And the cover life
Hides the wicked life
But decaying worms
Can't hide.

They show themselves
By feeding off
The soul life
And the cover life
The wicked life
Bred the worms and
The soul life
Decays.

The wicked life
Assaults the cover life
And the cover life
Becomes inadequate
For the wicked life
Seeks to show itself
As the cover life
Decays.

The wicked life
Assaults all life
That it contacts
For it is not life
The wicked life
Is disguised as life
The wicked life
Is death.

Turn away
From the double life
For the double life
Always ends in death
All in decay
Can be restored
Be not a fool
Choose life.

The Passion Stated As Jazz

(A title some people will have to understand.)

"It is a terrible thing to be happy!
How pleased we are with it!
How sufficient we think it!
How, being in possession of the false
aim of life, happiness, we forget the true aim,
duty!" - Victor Hugo, Le Miserables

The act of pain is received and self
gifted through the anguished response to love

to and through the father.

This love bleeds through the descending veil of
administered forty nine stripes. Our only hope

our only chance for salvation is gifted us and

we perhaps mistake it for a ticket to happy town. He died
to make us happy is the catch phrase

we dare not speak or even consciously

acknowledge less we find ourselves seeing ourselves our
true selves in the mirror of the

Word. Christian means "Little Christ" but where

is our Gethsemane our Calvary our ugly place of the
skull where we forsake this merry go

round laughter and grinning containing joyless

happiness and money. Yes, we cannot forget the
money. Prosperity equals Holiness and this

Holiness is displayed in how we manicure our

front lawns to protect the property values and
important little sensibilities of the neighbors and

appear the good little Christian to the world.

This Jazz is a Cinderella song,
if the shoe fits put it on…

The act of pain through the anguished response to
love bleeding through the descending veil of

forty nine stripes.

This is the joy!
This is the duty!
This is the song!

This is and always has been our only freedom.

The Climber

(On observing Mt Everest)

Why does one press to climb?
Enduring raw tortured skin
while lungs gasp needle thin air.
Your bones ache with stress and fatigue.
The pain, the peril
ever deepen,
press the soul.

"Because it's there," notwithstanding,
it is madness to be sure,

especially because you are not the first.

I press my soul to climb.
My skin is shredded, and my
lungs inhale stabbing torment.
These bones cry and bend to breaking.
The pain, the peril
ever deepen,
press the soul.

Calvary is for the climbing,
never madness to be sure,

especially because I am not the first.

The Romans 7:15-29 Blues

(These are the words. Your faith is the music.)

That thing I do, I wish I would not do.
That thing I do, I wish I would not do.
I guess my flesh gives nothin but the blues.

That thing I don't do, I wish I would do.
That thing I don't do, I wish I would do.
I wish that someone could give me good news.

I am no good, I am a messed up wretch.
I am no good, I am a messed up wretch.
This body I carry is full of death.

Who can save me from this body of mine?
Who can save me from this body of mine?
I think I'll call up Jesus on the line.

Said my flesh died with Jesus on his tree.
Said my flesh died with Jesus on his tree.
When I believe that word that's victory!

I am no longer deaths unwilling slave.
I am no longer deaths unwilling slave.
Thanks be to God Christ has declared me saved.

Since Jesus gave me all of this good news.
Since Jesus gave me all of this good news.
I must rename this poem, it aint the blues.

Angel Eyes

Bubbling laughter, a flashing smile, and eyes that light up her father. At four this girl feels like a superhero, her power, she makes her daddy smile.

One of her mother's coworkers almost invited her family to church, but got cold feet about talking religion on the job. She also decided that to go to that part of town would be way out of the way for a busy Sunday morning.

Velvet skin, long pig tails and, eyes that look for her father. At eight this girl is still a superhero but daddy is no longer around to be affected by her powers.

A pastor almost set up and evangelistic tent in her neighborhood but after a protracted business meeting with the deacons decided instead to fulfill his promise of remodeling the restrooms in the basement of the church.

Tomboy legs, singing dimples and, eyes that gobble up the morning. At twelve her powers affect substitutes, older boys introduce themselves, and young men circle closer.

Two church members saw her walking with friends from school and scolded her intensely about the length of her skirt and the tightness of her blouse. They did not however invite her to church or consider her mother's ability to keep a growing young girl in clothes that fit.

A little girl's voice, a woman's face and, eyes that recede from tomorrow. At sixteen this girl has lost all her super powers, for these men that come will sometimes laugh, but never do they smile.

Three hypocrites, doing the damage that hypocrites do, saw her walking one cool evening. She took their money like *anybody else's, but decided that she would not visit that church anymore for fear she might be recognized.*

A little girl's face, a woman's voice, and eyes that are brightened by her father. At twenty she has discovered late, but it is never too late, that though her daddy is still gone, her father never left and when she seeks his face she always finds a smile.

Angel eyes sharing her father's smile.

My Poetry

I am not
nor am I striving
to be
sufficiently nonspecific   or
poetically vague,
toying with the truth
as a kitten with
an expired
mouse.

I am
and I am striving
to be
sufficiently specific   and
caustically direct.
Mine is not the kitten
but the lion
doing battle for the truth
as its only means of
sustenance.

I haven't seen anybody vaguely
pulled from a burning building.
I haven't seen anybody nonspecifically
warned that they were walking off a cliff.

I cannot waltz the truth in ballroom fashion.
I must the dance of Jacob,
and I've got the limp to prove it.

Mine is not
the saccharin taste
of the rose colored glass.

Mine is
the taste of blood
from a ruptured lip
in the fifteenth round.

In the fifteenth round
there is no time
for vagueness.

Two Good Versions

Be not deceived;
God is not mocked:
for whatsoever a man soweth,
that shall he also reap.

For he that soweth
to his flesh
shall of the flesh
reap corruption;
but he that soweth
to the spirit
shall of the spirit reap
life everlasting.

Galatians 6:7-8
KJV (King James Version)

Or

Don't play yourself;
cause God cannot be played:
how you step to God,
is how God will step to you.

If you come wrong
it ain't gone be nice;
but if you come right
God will have your back
forever.

Galatians 6:7-8
KIRV (Keeping It Real Version)

Choice

Our lives are the reflections
Of the choices that we make
And these choices shape our lives.

How and where we are at this point
Of living life is the complete
And sum total of these choices.

Unforeseen circumstance present
Themselves to all but our choices
Will create new circumstance to choose.

Circumstance can be hardship and
Create pain but Godly choices
Will create Godly circumstance.

Choosing a circumstance only
To avoid Godly choices earns
Hardship in future circumstance.

Hardships earned or unearned always
Submit to Godly choices God
Works such circumstance for our good.

Our lives are the reflections
Of the choices that we make
And God's gift of choice gives life.

Hardness of Heart

Matt19:8

As I caress my memories of us
I am again startled by the murdered
marriage freshly dripping from stained hands.

Far far away in once upon a time
we mingled together, living, existing as one.
Now we mingle our fault
as we end our loving life.

One of us has stopped loving,
living, heeding God's voice,
and before there came these symptoms
there came hardness of heart.

If two will hear God
then
love will overcome.
If one heart remains
hard
there is nothing
to be done.

Love

God is Love.
If God is not present
then Love is not present.
If God is not honored
then Love is not honored.
You cannot express Love through sin
any more than you can express God through sin.

Love is an attribute
not an emotion.
Love flows from the spirit of God
through our spirits
and is expressed by our soul.
To express Love
is to express God.
Love is not emotional feeling.
A mother can feel,
anger, fear, joy, happiness, disappointment and more for her child
and never have her Love change.
Love is something other than feeling.
Love is an attribute
not an emotion.

You can always see if there is Love.
If there is no respect
then there is no Love.
When we substitute Love with emotion
then emotion substitutes respect with fear
and or admiration.
Fear and admiration is based on feelings.
Respect is given with Love.
Fear and admiration you have to earn
and is felt by the one who makes you earn it.
Respect is given when Love is given

and is separate from any feelings.
Fear and admiration is based on the worthiness of the receiver.
Respect is based on the worthiness of the giver.
If you are respected then you are held in high esteem through Love.
If you are not respected then you have to earn fear and or admiration through emotion.
This is how you can see if there is true Love;
if there is no respect then there is no Love,
just emotion.

If we walk in the spirit and not the flesh
then we walk in Love and not emotions.
If we do not walk in God then we do not walk in Love.
If we say "I Love you," and do not walk in God then we lie.
If we do not walk in God we tell the truth when we say
I emotion you.

Brothers and Sisters
Seek the Love of God.

To Her Who Has No Name
(Proverbs: 11:22)

Stately, elegant,
beautiful, smooth
as a ring of Gold,
in polished perfection.

At first glance
one wouldn't see
that
she no longer
knew herself.
She no longer
was herself.

At second glance
we notice
lingered covert glances,
appointments under radar.

It would seem
she has swallowed
the lie
that she is nothing
more than
face body
as
men flatter
with using and
discarding
like generic toilet paper
until again they desire
flesh smear.

What word will
make you see,

what phrase will
make you know
that
the Christ that
loves you real
can return to you
your name?

Until you heed
that Godly word,
that prophetic phrase.

You are moved

as a ring of gold
in a swine's snout
thus.

Self Portrait

Do you know who you are?
I have been a wonderful success.
I have been a horrible failure.
I see myself a blessing too many.
I see that by me not one of them is blessed.
There are many who are able to speak well of me.
There are many who are able to speak ill of me.
I think I understand the condition of my nature.

Do you know who you are?

I look into the mirror.
I study my pain.
The deeper I study the more pain I see.
When I try to look away, none of this can help me.

Who are you looking for?

In the mirror
I hope
One day to see
A very small part
Of a poor reflection
Of the only reflection
That is you.

Peace! You are not who you have been thus far,
Neither are you, who you think you to be,
Nor are you who others hear and or see.
You are all of who I speak that you are.

But I…

Peace.

Faith yes.

Seven Poem

1
Brown leaves fall from old
oak. Air is warm in sun, breeze
whispers jagged ice.

2
Bright eyed newlyweds
laugh, hold hands, and know no thing,
but a forever.

3
Antique old man bends
on aged church pew, face carved in
solemn contentment.

4
Christmas subtracts ma's
peach cobbler. Granddaughter's smile
reflects in pie pans.

5
A teenage knife glints
under red moon. Mother waits
in door, heart praying.

6
Hearing gospel heals
like liquid love. Drowned swine lie
prostrate on cliffs shore.

7
Even warm lives know
jagged whispers. Miracle!
Jesus makes life sweet.

My Mother’s Poem

(For Dorothy M. Harper)

Her life breathes beauty
strength to all who perceive her
move in silent victory
overcoming thus
unseen mountains with her love
joy laughter loving children
sharing life’s most pure
and affirming legacy
unassuming power her
gift to those willing
worthy to receive perceive
her triumphant love filled life.

The Seven Sonnets of Judas

The Feet of Judas (1)

I must the hiding feet of Judas wash.
Though heart be crushed by loved one's calloused heal
This pain that God as well as I do feel,
Is used to slay my flesh on daily cross.
Be not deceived my Lord will not be mocked.
Though wicked schemes do shape me in his love.
The schemers still will reap from God above,
For sowing to the flesh among his flock.
I must in love the steps of Jesus take
By serving those who kiss me to betray.
This love sincere and full of grace will make
Them choose Christ side or will push them away.
If I refuse to wash the filthy sod,
I lie if I say I am serving God.

Judas Still (2)

Is not this one a Judas still; who lies
With loveless wickedness; who tells our God
He is his own while playing in the sod
Of sin; our Lord afresh to crucify?
Is not this one a Judas still; who yields
His heart to envy, hatred, pride and strife;
Who will not yield his fleshly soul to Christ;
Yet claims a Holy ministry to build?
Among disciples faithful Judas walks
And does not hesitate to now betray;
Betrayal with a lifestyle that will block
Those trying to see Jesus on the way.
If we will not forsake the filthy dross,
We nail the Christ afresh upon the cross.

How the Judas Follows (3)

Forsaking all the Judas follows Christ.
Forsaking all; but not believing truth.
The words and deeds of Jesus are not proof
Enough to purchase pearl of a great price.
His eyes see what is carnal from the start.
His lamps give only darkness to his soul.
As others sacrifice for truth they know,
The alabaster box enrages heart.
His will and words of Jesus must collide.
His inner guile starts leaking to his walk.
It starts with robbing the bag on the side.
It ends with thirty pieces silver talk.
The Judas won't take Jesus at his word.
His self-betrayal is the last thing heard.

Grace For the Judas (4)

We all must love the Judas till the end.
Christ showed this love by giving him the sop.
Christ suffers long with all souls he has bought.
Gives miles of loving mercy to his friends.
The Judas must be given strong rebuke
By seeing the Christ likeness that we live;
A life proclaiming mercy and does give
An open door for him to follow suit.
As water soaks a sponge but flows past stone,
Christ love that fills the heart will not know guile.
Then enters evil to the heart unknown.
Perdition's son has walked his final mile.
The Judas ignores Gods extended grace,
Like Noah's world there is no hiding place.

Judas's Chosen Destiny (5)

The Judas now hangs strangely from a tree,
Though offered life receiving only death;
His eyes glazed open finding still no rest;
God swore in wrath that this is what would be.
Though silent Judas speaks to passersby:
"Be holy, thorns and briers do not bear!
The sacrifice of Jesus love with care!
Do not the Lord afresh to crucify!
God's mighty hands make straight the crooked way;
To fall in such while treading on his grace
Is fearful thing for judgment will repay,
And in his peace you will not see his face!"
Look deep upon this Judas on his tree;
Take care that there is not of him in thee.

Releasing the Judas (6)

I will not mourn the Judas for his choice.
Such mourning is accusing God of wrong.
Yes judgment fell but mercy suffered long.
If I am God's I must stand with his voice.
God's voice of judgment speaking only this;
To let him pour his own cup till it filled,
And let him drink the cup of his free will;
The enemy taking his heart in fist.
This Judas end may pain our loving hearts.
We see our former brother's life a waste.
Christ ministry was his to take a part.
This heavens gift despised with faithless taste.
I will not mourn this Judas timely death,
Believing God is good I'll take my rest.

Jesus Unhindered (7)

The Judas gone has left an empty space.
It will be filled by God and not by man.
Men casting lots will not undo God's plan.
The Judas by unlikely choice replaced.
At first Paul will be humbled by God's light;
Then unlike Judas Jesus words obey.
Forsaking his old life his debts are paid;
God's mercy and forgiveness gives new sight.
Who Judas for the thirty pieces sold,
And trodden under foot his heart to rend;
Who Paul counted more valuable than gold;
This Jesus will discern the hearts of men.
Right now your heart is bare before his face.
Are you a one that Jesus must replace?

Islands

Sometimes my brother does not smile at me,
though I extend my hand to his
over and over again
sometimes he does not smile at me.

When he does not smile at me I say...
"Let Chloe's house report no contentions among us.
There is no need for us to fight denomination against denomination. My brother, let us reason together on one accord."

If he still does not smile at me I say...
"Pay no attention to the color of my skin my brother,
my friend. God does not care if I am darker or perhaps lighter than you. It is of no consequence for we are all members of the same Holy nation and ours is the common blood of Christ."

If he still does not smile at me I say...
"Do not attempt to look down on me if I am a woman for God has said there is no longer Jew nor Greek, slave nor free, male nor female
for Christ is all and in all."

If he still does not smile at me I say...
"Selfish ambition and petty attitudes have no place in God's plan for this is God's ministry. My brother, my loved one, I will serve you gladly for the greatest of all must be the servant of all therefore turn your anger aside."

If he still does not smile at me, I say...
"Take no heed to those who say that I am poor and not worthy of a place among you. Do not look at my inexpensive clothes and frown. We are both part of the same royalty and salvation is not a matter of outward appear-

ance."

If he still does not smile at me...
With a tear in my eye and "praise the Lord" on my lips I shake the dust from my feet and trod the heavy path to reluctant isolation.

And then...my brother smiles at me.

Haiku Sketches

"God Bless You!" should have
balm on the tip instead of
sharp points all around.

Today's sacrifice;
not bulls or rams but only
a few hours ' sleep.

Jesus knows me still
he sends to me no letter
of resignation.

Pharisee gags his
beliefs down the throat of one
who would taste Jesus.

Sex sin is shard from
early pain, anger, doubt, fear.
Our cracked childhood screams.

Eternity weeps
on a tall blue sunny day.
Souls drop like hung men.

God moves through our life
as trainer, coach, advocate...
Race hard for the prize.

A Tale of Two Sisters

Ann came out to bible study.
Missy stayed at home.
Missy called Ann a "Busy Body"
When Missy got on the phone.

Missy stayed home for Tuesday night prayer,
Ann was there every week.
Ann was real sweet to folk everywhere.
Missy could barely speak.

Ann thanked God for what she had,
But Missy complained for more.
Ann blessed those that had it bad,
But Missy locked up her door.

It was time for blessings to come
And Ann received from her master.
Missy can't make the devil run
And put the blame on her pastor.

Now imagine this if you will
A clear mirror in your right hand,
Who is it that you are seeing,
Sister Missy or sister Ann?

Ma Boo

(For Mother Bentley)

The first time that I saw her there was fire
And love and that mixture moved throughout the
Room blessing all that would receive from Christ.

A college dorm is the last place you would
Expect a mother in Zion to move
Freely, unfettered, fire love flowing.

Mixed with humor and her infectious smile
Was a strong dose of truth, conviction, and
Encouragement. God's love personified.

Years later this ministry was flowing
Undimmed as I sat at her hospital
Bed. "Son, iron wears out. God didn't call you

To everything ministry. Even our
Lord took time to rest. You can work yourself
To death if you want to but these saints will

Replace you and in six months half of them
Won't remember your name. God has worked it
Out that if you take time to rest the church

Around the world will survive for one day."
I am rescued by a nurse who stops in
The doorway. She sees me and hesitates.

"It's ok baby you need me?" The nurse
Answers: "It wasn't that important I
will stop again before my shift is up."

"Sweet girl, just needs Jesus love." She holds my
Eyes in hers. "Just about finished my course.
I have got just a few more days to work,

But you still have work to do, pace yourself.
Now stop that sad face at the truth. We both
Know that this body is just about done.

Son, though this earthy tabernacle be
Dissolved I have a building eternal
In the heavens. I'm ready, let me go.

My savior got me out of the junk pile
And put me in heavenly places with
Him. My life has been good and now heaven!

Now you need to consider that it might
Be important for folk to see how I
Die, they have already seen how I lived."

I see the wisdom in her words, she served
Her Lord, her pastors and church family
touching hundreds and through them thousands.

I rise to leave and she takes my hand. "Son
When you meet me in heaven we will have
A time! But don't you rush to get there. Rest!"

I smile and nod through the clouds in my eyes.
"Son, I love you but Jesus loves you more."
Around me flaming love swirls and strengthens.

My smile broadens despite myself. She gives
Her signature wink and nod and that smile.
"If you see that nurse tell her to come in."

She went home to be with her Lord two days
Later. At her home going the tears where
Mine but the smile was the one she gave me.

In this life she loved freely, smiled often,
Ministered Christ graciously and was loved.

Who Else but God?

I look to thee my God
To keep me on the path
This narrow path I trod
No other help I have

Who else but you can know
This weary pain I feel
You fight my wicked foe
You feed my soul its meals

There is no other place
My lonely soul can hide
And when I seek your face
You're always by my side

So when my knees grow weak
None else but you I seek

Eutychus

(Acts 20:7-12)

He was in a place,
a lofty place,
full of light and truth
and that warm family feeling.

He, like too many others,
was drawn to the outer edges
of what he failed to see was life;
the only life there is,
the only life there ever will be.

Becoming bored with the life
he perched in the window
to watch the world go by,
and in the watching
was enticed into a sleep;
the sleep of the world,
the sleep of the blind.

First came the sleep,
then came the fall;
the fall from the lofty place,
the fall to the world below.

Praise be to God for the Called of God
who can snatch from blindness,
who can snatch from death,
the ones who fall to the world below.

And Eutychus, sweet Eutychus,
angel touched one thousand times upon
his face and cheek;
though he fell to the world dead
was taken home alive
to live again in the lofty place.

Watch closely the windows
for the world still calls.

We must keep him awake!
We must keep them awake!
Our Eutychus.

Hypocrite

Wickedness glazed with
name and reputation of
God that won't be mocked.

I Am Afraid

Afraid for slaves of the polite world's vice
Who learn what to serve in cold worldly pews
Where taught to fit in like so many screws
Discarding away that pearl of great price.
Afraid for those who try to serve the Lord
By mowing their lawns keeping them so nice
And gifting orphans once a year or twice
But their hearts belong to this fallen world.
Afraid to serve this systems fallen mind
Which shapes this world in anger and in pain,
Who without Christ has rendered all men blind
And caused their hearts to carry common stain.
We should not be afraid of this world scorn
But living as though Christ has not been born.

The Eyes Have It.

The lamp of the body
is the eyes,
not the lamp of the soul,
not the Lamp of the Spirit,
but the lamp of the body.

If our eyes
(sought after desire,)
is good
then the whole body
(affections, appetites, self-protections,)
will be full of light.

But if our sought after desire
(our eyes)
lingers on, hesitates over, drinks in
darkness
then our
affections, appetites, self-protections
(body)
will be full of darkness.

Job made a covenant with his eyes,
a deal with his lamp:
"I won't let you linger on sin
and you won't fill my body with darkness."

We say we are what we eat,
but rather we are
(affections, appetites, self-protections,)
what we see.

When the pressure is on
it reveals us.
when we are hurt, frightened, pressed,
where do our eyes

turn?

Where our eyes turn
under pressure
tells us what we really are,
what we really love.

Jesus uses pressure
to turn our eyes
toward him,
and he is the light.

He fills our bodies
with himself,
and in him is no darkness at all.

The lamp of the body
is the eyes.

Keep your lamp full of light,
your body full
of Jesus.

Lyric

It's for them we should be praying,
They are ones who say, "We Hate!"
The most tragic way of saying
That my hurt or fear is great.

Tribulation Earthquake Poem

Silla bowls of wrath (this scrib
And) cause dee saken , of world is
Pray king will cause the fall(Lo) (lower)
And come ing a part , of (B) earth
Surf us writ hing down cit (y) vents
Somemo k ings in world.

Cup fools of wrath stag her and poor.
Ow tt confuse (is)say won t under
Stand under dee p resser long. (Thoughts and)
Real iland(tys) our sunk k an da get d ark
Said No ah but it is go na ll red y
F(l)ew a way for son(m). people is cape
Canaveral raptur . ning WO ver a
Knew lie ff . for eny lef (t)ribula shun
The truth. sh hell fish, people cook th him
Near Wo shun or in lake . afire Wo nttake A long
time. Seconds (de ath) is all.

Judgment Jezebel

(2nd Kings 9:30-37, Rev 2:20-23)

Attached to perceived influence
you quiver and taste blood
like yesterday's leech.

A web of ugliness dances around you.
Within these controls and lying affections
the innocent are consumed at your leisure.

Those who practice the perceived weaknesses
love, goodness, mercy, submission
earn your hard eyed malice,
your cruelly laughing contempt.

Truth will always destroy you
therefore you kill the prophets,
preserving your deception,
gateway to your lair.

But, Elijah has survived.

Your religion proves false!
Jehu at the window!
The eunuchs cast down their chosen bondage!

You are hillside dog dung, save...
Hands that took hold of folly.
Feet that pursued wickedness.
Scull that carried angry seductions.

Warnings of the judgment Jezebel.

You have been given space.
You have chosen.
You will receive.

The Idea

Son of Man, Jesus
triumphant walk on the sea,
bidding me to come.

Through A Glass Darkly

(1 Corinthians 13:12)

Salty tears run swiftly
Like hot wax down a burning candle.
Your problems loom large;
Shadowing your peace of mind,
There is no natural hope to turn to;
But victory is already yours,
And hope has always been yours,
For the spirit has hope
All its own
And this is what we live on.

See Jesus, our sweet Jesus,
Through the tender veil
Of the darkened glass
For this is what we live on.

Monotone hellos and goodbyes move dryly
Like rancid dust over cold concrete.
These people pass you coolly
And sometimes they lash out.
Some people of this world our cold and cruel
And nothing in your flesh wants to love them;
But then you love them anyway
And feel a joy in doing it,
For the spirit has love
All its own
And this is what we live on.

See Jesus our sweet Jesus,
Through the tender veil
Of the darkened glass
For this is what we live on.

Sweet hallelujahs flow freely
Like maple syrup over warm pancakes.
The worship is high and moving higher still,
We bask in joy unspeakable
And praise the name of God.
There is nothing our eyes see
That can make us feel this way,
But we see Jesus sweetly
And sweeter shall we see him,
For the spirit has sight
All its own
And this is what we live on.

See Jesus, our sweet Jesus,
Through the tender veil
Of the darkened glass
For this is what we live on.

Homeless Scream

The heart of God weeps.
Soft snow harsh on cardboard roof.
Torn plastic screams ice.

Grate sleeper in the
shadow of our hearts gravestone.
Our seared conscience screams.

Homeless flower screams
silent lament on tip toe,
"Where is my Christian!?"

I scream you scream we
all scream for ice scream, but now...
homeless scream at us.

The Condition Our Condition Is In

The majority says little, much says the frenzied few.
Hidden little babies killed by hidden little choices;
Hushed from this world but not mute, we are deaf to
their voices.
In heaven do you think these babies cheer our right to
choose?
Young girl abused grows unhealed and is left without
defense.
Chooses lifestyle and is used as a recruiting example.
A young boy chooses same as former victim has ample
Cover to plunder that hurting soul of its innocence.
There must be something someone could be doing for
them girl.
Well yea, I'd like to help them, if anyone really can,
But our budget isn't big enough for reaching the world.
There's no time, Friday got to check out this new
Christian band.
Our ears become deaf blind and hollow our poisoned
dead eyes
When we sacrifice our mission for worldly compromise.

Apology

Marriage is the union of two souls,
bone of bone,
flesh of flesh,
two souls blended in love,
and
    God
        Is
          Love.
Without God means without love.
All that remains is fleshly emotion,
soulish feeling.

How can two walk together
unless they agree,
Godly love to Godly love
or
fleshly emotion to fleshly emotion?

When a man finds a wife
he has found a good thing,
she becomes the man's choice,
the man's responsibility.

When seeking to choose a wife
a man must first seek God,
forsaking all fleshly emotion,
learning Godly love from the Father
as he is instructed by the word.

If a man does not seek God,
but chooses from fleshly emotion
then love will be absent from the marriage
in the man and or the wife.

If the marriage then is shipwrecked
it is the man's responsibility,
for it is the man who chooses wife,
how and why his choice was made
belongs only to the man.

Therefore

the wife must be loved of the man
as the church is loved of Christ,
from Gethsemane to Golgotha
until his flesh is crucified.

Then

the man can say to the father
"Tetelestai" (It is finished),
gifting his wife his sacrifice
to be cherished or rejected
embraced or cast away.

But

whether cherished or rejected
the man is still responsible
for every wrong done in his marriage.

So

I apologize.
I, apologize to you.
I apologize for every hurt, betrayal, deception
I have done
to me
of you.

Daddy

Daddy I can't see you
I see...the fixed bikes, the rescued cat,
that bit through your glove.
I see...the trips to the park
where we all posed on the plastic
pony, like clowns at a circus rodeo.
They are gone
from memory
save the faded
pictures
that we took.
And they are...
fading...
still.

We
don't
talk.
Daddy I can't hear you.
I hear... the rumbling of the truck that took us giggling
and wide eyed
to the airport to watch the planes take off.
I hear the rushing of the wind
from the engines
that blew hot
air into my face,
and sent
Clarence and I laughing
and stumbling
down
the sidewalk trying to
out run
my cap.
I hear... the monkeys in your truck
that were supposed to go straight
from the airport to the zoo

but you stopped
at home
so that we could see them,
and become celebrities with all the other
seven and nine year olds.
We have grown...
long past...
nine or celebrities
and we are
growing
still.

We
don't
talk.
Daddy I can't feel you.
I feel...the hurt in your voice
when you proclaim,
"I'm an army man,"
and you remember how life was
and you see
how it is today.
I feel... the hurt of a former Staff Sergeant M.P.
when he is told he is a half inch
too short for a civilian police force.
I feel...your hurt as a man dies when he runs his car
under your truck and your job is lost
because your truck
is parked at the
local...
beer...
garden...

We
don't
talk.
Daddy I can't see hear feel you,
save for dry recollection.

Is it the alcohol that I see drain
your soul away like so much water
in a pay toilet,
or is it the scars of teasing
I took when I was young
and all the children knew
that my father was drunk again,
or was it spilled sheet cake on Clarence's birthday.
Even then I perceived...
knew...
saw,
that your hurt was deeper than ours,
but young boys are so unforgiving of
unperfected fathers.
You say
we
don't
talk
I think it's rather we can't talk.
There is a wall within
that I have not let Jesus
break down
and when out of your need
you told me
you loved me
the wall came up
and would not
let me
speak.
We will talk,
I mean really talk,
but today all that I have
to offer...
I offer
right now.

In the name of Jesus
I claim our healing,
and I love you.
I always have.
Forgive me
please
forgive me.

Restoration
(In three Poems)

Conviction

Aloneness covers you blanket like-cold.
There are many lies but the one
you struggle hardest not to believe
is that you are utterly forsaken,
unloved by God or man.

Hold on
        fellowship
                    embrace the word and…
hold on!

Hope

You believe that God
is with you. You know
that you have help,
and at the far end
of the cold moss covered tunnel
there is now the promise
of light.

Move forward
              lift your head
                            strengthen your back
and…
move forward!

Deliverance

There is light.
Light that fills every aspect

of your life, every pore of your being,
the light of deliverance.
You add to it with rejoicing and
praise, and are lifted to gossamer
heights and joy unspeakable.

Your restoration is at hand,
even when you think
you have fallen beyond help

hold on
        move forward
                      for…
your restoration
is at hand!

On Seeking Enlightenment

Back in the day when
I was seeking enlightenment
I kept my ear to the ground listening
for all the newest and deepest ideas.

I could quote you the top five physical
and spiritual reasons why you shouldn't eat pork.

I conversed freely about some who have thirty three degrees of knowledge and others who have three hundred and sixty degrees.

I read every book on Zen from "Zen in the Art of Archery" to "Zen in the Art of Motorcycle Maintenance."

I could converse about politics, mysticism and jazz all in the same paragraph and still maintain
that philosophical deep look.

I applauded the musicians that performed life's questions as though they had all the answers.

I read from Oliver Wendell Holms to St Augustine and made them all fit into my unique little philosophy of life.

I would quote things like, "If one asked of the truth and another told him you can be sure that neither had knowledge about the nature of truth."

I had the respect of all the hip cats and heavy dudes who could likewise philosophize with the best of them.

I, with my fellow sophist, were led into deep complexities, that I took for simplicities, and a detailed exploration of my own natural instincts.

Yet in all of this there was always
something missing. Even when the social,
political and philosophical thing fit snugly
together there was this unexplainable vacantness.

It would seem that the whole was less
than the sum of all those individual parts.

Then, like a salmon returning to its birth stream
I returned to my early training,
namely my mother's relationship with God.
Her midnight prayers her sincere faith
was like a beacon that provided warm memories
of strength, peace and precious contentment.

Then early one morning
not far from Damascus road
the scales fell from my eyes.

Now one surrender, one baptism
And one filling of the Holy Spirit later
I can say the truth,
the whole truth and
nothing but the truth
in three words
three times and
in three seconds.

Jesus is Lord!
Jesus is Lord!
Jesus is Lord!

Invitation

The fire roared in love and power,
And from the bush proclaimed the hour
That salvation now was close at hand,
And the Lord himself would make the stand.

Holy fire,
Eternal fire,
Fire of healing,
Fire of cleansing,
The Lord our God will baptize you with fire.

The fire calls and burns and moves,
To reach the lost and proclaim the news
That all who see they will receive.
The fire burns eternally.

Holy fire,
Eternal fire,
Fire of healing,
Fire of cleansing,
The lord our God will baptize you with fire.

The fire burns away the fake
With power that can surly make
A new life that he freely gives,
Come now partake of God and live.

Holy fire,
Eternal fire,
Fire of healing,
Fire of cleansing,
The Lord our God will baptize you with fire.

What I Have Come To Know

(For my sisters, a journey to psalm 91:1)

When I came to know
That he did not love me now
My sun grew dim
Graying a daily walk
That I no longer chose to lift
Into the joy of believing God
And all my times swirled downward
Into a numb and cold existence

When I came to know
That he never did love me
I embraced an empty promise
With desperate gifts of flesh
(I was a useful fool)
My gifts could make him love me
I believed this in my head
Though my heart had told me no

When I came to know
That he was cruel and would not love me
I stumbled down and wept
For my love had been impossible
Another self-delusion
Mirage of thirsty soul

When I came to know
The pain of a lonely heart
Anger and hardness took me
So I played the familiar game
Trading flesh for lying affections
Living a life of need
In desperate compromise
Showing all a clowns painted smile
Hiding even from myself

But

When I came to know
That I was really loved of Jesus
I dwelled in His secret place
He wiped away my tears
And called me His beloved
I no longer played the game
Smiling falsely as a clown

This love in His secret place
I had never known before
In peace I was brightly covered
Lighting my daily walk
And lifting it on high

When I came to know
That all I need is Jesus
And the plans He has for me
Are for good and not for evil
For He has the man who loves me
Seeking diligently for me
When I have been prepared
This man He has will find me

I rest now in the promise
And joy of believing God
This is the secret place
That I have come to know

Haiku Definitions

Poiema (Workmanship) (Eph2:10)

Crafted expression
of God. We are his love poem,
wooing wayward world.

Grace (Heb 12:28)

God's love expressed as
personality; working
in, for, and through us.

Holiness (Rom 12:1)

Escapes perfection's
hopelessness by living
body sacrifice.

Faith (Hab 2:4)

Saying yes when your
will, intellect, emotion,
say no to your God.

Sons of God (1John 3:1-3)

God's genderless term
of endearment, bequeathing
our role in the earth.

Christmas Haiku

His birth ascends through
crimsoned dark walled tomorrow.
Let all earth rejoice.

Thoughts and Ruminations

1

A Mother is angry. This mother's son is attending a church of another denomination. Her son and a boy from this other church met at school and became friends. Her son enjoys the other church more than the one he grew up in. She does not trust that other church. If she fails her son may become a passionate witness for Christ at that other church. If she fails her son will not necessarily be shot.

Another mother is angry. Her son refuses to attend any church, anywhere, at any time. If she fails her son may be shot in a drive by shooting.

In this way, their worlds are different.

2

God is not a good fortune teller, He does not look into the future, He does not look into the past. God sees and abides in all time at the same time. God lives in the infinite present, which is eternity, as well as every part of the linear progression known as time. Therefore God sees all of time and everything that has and will happen much like we look at a map of the world. God sees the beginning and end of great roads of history, boarders of change, intersections of conflict and more. The most important to him are small, short side streets.

Your life is a small, short side street.

3

Pharisees, Sadducees, and Teachers of the Law have taught us many lessons. One of the most important lessons is that religion and or religious culture can live separate from, antagonistic to or even the enemy of the life of Christ.

Many churches continue this lesson today.

4

When we first come to God he follows us and is with us always, no matter where we go or what we do he loves us and ever desires to be closer to us and bless us. In all things he was crucified for us.

Then things may change.

If our love for God becomes deep enough we follow him and are with him always. No matter where he goes or what he does we love him and are ever desiring to be a blessing to him. In all things we are crucified with him.

The second way is more excellent than the first I think.

5

A pastor must grow his church. He recruits Christians from other churches. He recruits people from the world he is familiar with. He studies the latest business models. He drives past the crack house every day.
They are not good recruits neither are they mentioned in his business model. They have not been invited. They are in very good company. The spirit of God has also not been invited.

6

I once owned a dog that was known as a fear biter. Fear biters are dogs that are insecure and therefore always intimidated by people and other dogs. This makes them unnecessarily dangerous and destructive because they will attack innocent people and dogs based on their own unwarranted fears. These dogs always feel vulnerable and threatened even when no threats exist. They are especially dangerous when facing the unfamiliar or something they do not understand. A fear biter that perceives a nonexistent threat will attack viciously to protect itself and its territory.

Note to self: I must always and in every way endeavor to be better than a frightened dog.

7

Christians, the really good ones, know better than and therefore take great care not to be associated with, be seen in the company of, or risk their reputation with the sexually immoral, drunkards, thieves or anyone else of ill repute. In this way Christians, the really good ones, know better than Jesus, who had the unfortunate circumstance of being called the friend of tax collectors and sinners.

8

Augustine is intelligent. Augustine has studied many books for many years and has many answers. One of Augustine's answers is that if there is a God at best he can only be understood through a complicated philosophical journey and at worst is unknowable. Augustine is not aware that he and his books have found many answers, but that none of these answers spring from the correct questions. Many years later, Augustine has become St Augustine and he says, "Understanding is the reward of faith. So seek not to understand that you may believe but believe that you may understand." In this statement we see that St Augustine has learned the most important question and its answer.

9

The enemy of all souls works hard to shape this world in his image. The enemy of all souls also works very hard to disguise his hand in this shaping. This world provides more food than is needed but people go hungry. This world provides more land than is needed but we have war. This world kills adults and children with preventable diseases. This world provides humans with opportunities and training to perform limitless forms of wickedness and cruelty from our early life to our death bed. In all the history of humanity we have never been able to slow, much less stop, this systematic degradation.

The world as OZ...
Please pay attention to the mind behind the curtain.

10

See our God. He is laughing loudly. He is laughing in heaven and he is also here on earth. The nations are very angry. They are so angry that they point their water guns at God and squeeze the trigger. He laughs even more. The nations go into a rage. They call our God rude. They say that to laugh while someone is trying to disbelieve you is extremely impolite. They threaten to disbelieve him more and also to shoot him again. This makes God hysterical. He almost doubles over with laughter.
The nations have imagined a vain thing. They have

imagined that to disbelieve God is to make him not exist. So they wave their water guns violently and disbelieve harder. This makes God slap his knee and vibrate laughing. Our God is laughing. Our God who longs to be their God is laughing.

Our God is laughing to keep from crying.

Mixed Nuts

Text from God:
You said OMG...Am I Really?

Biblical Tabloid:
Goliath was slung down in a run by stoning in the valley today by young David for dissing his peeps and their God.

We all live suspended in the narrow
space between one heart beat and eternity.

Oh God! Are you out there?!?!
No… I'm here with you.

I am soaked, proof that the rain falls on the just and the unjust. Proof that circumstance won't tell
me which one I am.

The Christian Equation:
(Jesus + relationship) x Love = Lifestyle

I claw at my Christian mask hoping to find underneath some expression of Jesus.

Twenty First Century Repentance:
I have just killed Uriah and plan to marry Bathsheba. Solution: I will never fail to attend church on Mother's Day again.

Note to Self:
You can pray on an airplane or you can read the emergency instructions on an airplane but apparently doing both at the same time really freaks people out.

Text from God:
I don't exist!?! LOL

Televangelist to Audience:
"Do I look like a man who could be trusted to provide your weekly loan shark?"

When I tell you I am Christian you pause
and I begin to glimpse the mob with their torches.

Note to Self:
We walk by faith and not by sight but God still expects you to look both ways before you cross the street.

A beautiful day, the birds are chirping, the bees are humming, the people are marrying and giving in marriage… and the clock is ticking.

Paradox:
God knows me completely.
God loves me completely.

Text from God:
HIT ME BACK!!!

"You need Jesus!" is a universal truth, not a left handed insult of character.

Children's Haiku
Jesus rules, devil
drools. Jesus is fun for me.
Loves like mom and dad.

II

OTHER RADICAL EXPLORATIONS

Short Observations on the Nature of Light

He is the King eternal, immortal, invisible.

Light is invisible. We cannot see light. We can only see what light touches and illuminates. The evidence that light is present is always and only the things light touches and illuminates. Outer space between our planet and the sun is full of sunlight, but it is dark. We cannot see this light. If we see a planet or a space craft or any object in space, then we see the evidence of the light that is always present, as the light illuminates the object that we see. Outer space is dark because it is a vacuum. It is a vast emptiness, and there is nothing in this vacuum or emptiness for light to touch and illuminate. If light cannot find anything to touch and illuminate, then there is darkness. Light will never cease to be light but if there is nothing it can touch then we will live in darkness and not perceive the light that is everywhere.

You are the light of the world.

Pure light contains all colors. These colors are in harmony and are not separate in pure light. Pure light can be fractured into a rainbow. This is the separation and deformity of the nature of pure light. Rainbow light is fractured and is very poor at touching and illuminating. Rainbow light does not reveal the true nature of things because each part of the rainbow is lacking every other part of itself. When a particular part of rainbow light touches something the illumination is tainted by its own color. A particular part of a rainbow colors everything after the nature of its own color therefore it does not reveal the true nature of the thing it touches. This is the difference between unified light and fractured light. Unified light reveals what is true, fractured light shows us only after its own color.

I*n him was life; and that life was the light of men.*

Light is necessary for life. If the world had no light, every living thing would die ,and nothing new would be born. Light gives life to every living thing, and, every living thing receives its life from light. If the world no longer had light, every plant and every animal would die. Even animals that live in total darkness and are blind ignoring and living as if there was no light, would die because everything that sustains them, everything they depend on, even though they are unaware of it, is sustained by light.

For He is the Lord, He does not change.

Light is not relative. Light does not change according to your perspective or from what place you observe it. Light travels at 299,792,458 meters per second in a vacuum and is observed at that speed from every perspective. If a car travels at 100 miles per hour and you travel next to that car at 75 miles per hour that car you are beside will only appear to pass you at 25 miles per hour. The car is traveling 25 miles per hour faster than you so its relative speed to you is 25 miles per hour. For light this is not so. If you travel very fast, even approaching the speed of light itself light will still appear to you to be traveling at 299,792'458 meters per second. Time and space will change around you to allow light to appear to you this way. Light does not change; it doesn't matter from where you observe it.

Light overcomes darkness.

Darkness cannot exist of its own but only in the absence of light. When light touches anything then darkness disappears. Darkness cannot overcome light and darken what light touches. Darkness can only cover something in the absence of light. Darkness cannot be measured. There is no speed of darkness. Darkness does not travel in waves or particles. Darkness does not have mass or energy. Darkness only exists and moves in the absence of something for light to touch. Light and darkness are not equally powerful. They do not compete with one another. Light's mere existence moves the darkness into non-existence. Light has no competition. Darkness is only the absence of light.

And the light shines in the darkness but the darkness did not comprehend it.

Light takes every opportunity to have access. Great pains have to be taken to exclude light and cultivate darkness. Light will take every opportunity, move through every crack or seem, to touch and illuminate. Light is also gentle. It will not force its way. If darkness is sought it can always be found. Dark places can be found or created away from the light because light will not force its way, but if light is carried into the dark place it will cease to be a dark place. That place will have light. To stay in darkness you must actively seek or create dark places and flee when light is brought to that dark place. It takes decisive action to stay in darkness. Light takes every given opportunity to touch and illuminate. Light constantly seeks to eliminate darkness but light is gentle it will not force its way.

God is light and in him is no darkness at all.

Yes God is light. As we understand the nature of physical light, we can begin to understand the nature of God who is spiritual light. God touches and illuminates. God unifies us as the light of the world and God's heart is broken when we are fractured from one another. God provides life and without God all flesh would die together. God does not change. God is the same yesterday, today, and forever. God overcomes darkness. Darkness has no power over God. Darkness exists in man because of God's mercy. God is always seeking to touch and illuminate the human heart. God will use even the smallest opportunity to touch us but God will not force his way.

Atheist Faith

I think I do not have enough faith to be an atheist. You see, I asked my friend the atheist why the universe is ordered. For example; why are the laws of physics constant when there is no scientific reason why they should be? Things in a vacuum fall to the earth at 32ft per second per second every time. Why wouldn't it fall 32ft per second per second one time and 4ft per second per second the next? It seems that in physics and everywhere else we look we find an imposed order, an unexplained uniformity.

My friend told me that the universe is not ordered but chaotic and that random variables come together to cause a constant rate of fall. Things fall at the same rate on earth because the earth displaces a constant amount of space, and causes a constant amount of gravity which results in the consistency of the fall. If you change any of the variables the rate of the fall will change. Order is the illusion of chaotic variables.

I told my friend that we should not be like the fish that cannot see what water is because it cannot see what water is not. The fish does not know what water is because it has always been surrounded by water and can not imagine a world outside of water. It is hard for us to see what order is because we have never seen what order is not. We have always been surrounded by order.

There is no scientific reason why any law of physics should behave the same way twice. Just because we have always observed these laws behaving consistently and have even worked out science based on these observations does not mean there is a scientific reason why they should.

Humans had always observed things fall to the earth but it was not until Sir Isaac Newton asked why that we began to explore the concept of gravity.

To date there is no scientific reason why the earth would displace a constant amount of space, why gravity would cause a constant pull and cause a thing to fall at a constant rate. All of these variables that come together are separate pieces of the same order. Whenever any of these variables or any law of physics behaves the same way constantly, it is obeying an imposed order and there is no scientific explanation why it should.

My friend told me that every indication is that the universe has always functioned this way since very shortly after the big bang and that there is an answer and one day science will discover it.

I then asked my friend the atheist what caused the big bang and what came before it.

He then explained to me that there are many theories about the big bang and the origin of the universe, but the most important idea for me to grasp is that time was probability created at the big bang as a part of our universe, so that our universe and time share the same beginning, and time is possibly limited to the outer edge of our finite universe as it expands. So there was technically no before the big bang since time did not exist.

I was not satisfied though and asked him if these various theories explained what caused time to suddenly appear out of eternity through the big bang.

He told me that string theory ,and its multiple dimensions can explain where time came from, and possibly what happened before it.

So I asked why did the dimensions explained by string theory suddenly create time and all the matter and enrgy in our universe through the big bang.

He then told me that there is a limit to how far back we can see and how much we can understand at this time, because life and mankind has only existed for a short time in our universe, not long enough to grasps everything from the start to finish.

So then I asked my friend the atheist how life came into existence. He then explained to me about the primordial pool, amino acid strings, solar ultraviolet energy and other things that seemed really scientific and important. That did not answer my question though. I wanted to know how an inanimate object becomes alive. How can a group of inanimate chemicals like amino acids that have no consciousness become animated and evolve a rudimentary survival instinct and begin to respond to its environment enough to do what is necessary to stay alive.

He explained to me about life precursors and DNA instructions in the most basic forms of life, but told me that we did not yet know and that one day science would give us an explanation.

So then I asked my friend the atheist how something as complex as DNA, could have been constructed randomly. It is hard to accept that billions of possible bases came together in exactly the correct sequence to create just the right nucleotides, and that these nucleotides out of all the possible alternatives would connect together in perfect order to form the exact working twisted double helix DNA strands to accidentally create sustainable life.

My friend told me that anything was possible given enough time and number of attempts. He then stated that a good way for me to understand this concept is the "Infinite Monkey Theorem." Simply put, this theorem states that mathematically if you have an infinite number of typewriters typed by an infinite number of monkeys, one of those monkeys would produce perfectly the complete works of Shakespeare. He said that no matter how complex something is, it can be randomly produced given the right set of circumstances.

I did not think his analogy was relevant since he had previously told me that this version of the expanding universe was finite in time and space, which means it would not allow infinite time or attempts. This means that he would have to have a finite group of monkeys with a finite number of typewriters, which changes his analogy. When you have an infinite number of anything, the math becomes completely different from math that does not deal with the infinite. For instance, if he gave me thirty percent of his infinite monkeys and typewriters, I would soon realize that I too had an infinite number of monkeys and typewriters and he would still have an infinite number of monkeys and typewriters, even though he had just given me thirty percent of his.

Infinity is a concept but does not exist in time or space. There is not an infinite amount of anything. In the realm of the finite however, even one monkey on one typewriter for every particle of the observable universe (ten to the eightieth power) typing one thousand key strokes per second for one hundred times the scientifically believed age of the universe (ten to the twentieth power) the chance of these monkeys creating any large part of any work of Shakespeare, not to mention the complete works, is just about impossible (approaches zero).

I also thought it was odd that he would use intelligent beings in his theorem, even if the intelligence of the monkeys did not approach Shakespeare's intelligence. It seems to me that any type of intelligence would pollute the outcome.

I thought a better analogy would be a finite number of tornadoes in a finite number of automobile factories creating a working car which is even less likely than his finite typing monkey theorem. He did not seem to like my tornado car theorem very much and told me that mere statistical mathematics, as it pertained to creation was not enough to shake his disbelief in God creating life.

I then told him that I thought all of his answers lacked the same thing, a first cause. I told him that I knew what the first cause was. He was not very interested and told me that he would hold on to his beliefs, as they were and one day if I really thought about it and was honest with myself that I would come to believe as he did.

Now that is great faith!

The Ant That Would Be King

Take a mind trip with me. No, not a drug induced purple haze mind trip mind you, but a mind trip induced from fresh air and a searching heart. A mind trip can be useless or we can learn something from it. You decide which type of mind trip this one is.

Imagine that ants from your backyard garden have invaded your house and what they don't know is that they are only days away from the exterminator. These ants were content to live in your backyard garden with all its juicy fruits and vegetables until a new leader ant from another anthill put himself in charge of the ants from your backyard. This ant knows just a little more than the other ants do and this ant doesn't want the ants to dig and aerate your soil or guard the garden from harmful insects. This ant has gone as far as to believe he should be in charge of the house and has convinced the other ants that they should have all those goodies from your kitchen.

The question is, how could we save these ants from the exterminator? Could we post a danger sign? No, a sign wouldn't help an ant. Could we seal the house? No, ants can always find a way into the house and therefore into death. If we spoke to the ants at the top of our voice would that help? No, ants couldn't begin to understand sound as language.

It seems that these ants our doomed.

The problem is ants don't live on our level. They couldn't even begin to understand a fraction of what we know. You couldn't teach an ant sound as language because they communicate by chemicals. If an ant is in danger it releases a chemical that whips the other ants into a frenzy to fight. If an ant finds food it releases a chemical that says food is found. The ant mind is small and limited to very basic things. You couldn't teach an ant to use a cell phone, to write poetry or to convey even simple ideas like yes or no to his fellow ants. You can't teach an ant any of the most basic things that you do every day. It is beyond them. To make things worse, the ant from the other anthill speaks their language. This ant has released a food chemical trail leading right into your kitchen. The ants from your backyard don't know what else to do so they follow the trail strait to their future destruction.

There is one thing that you can do though. You can become an ant yourself. It is really the only way to save them. If you, a human, become an ant you would still understand about exterminators and kitchens and could help the ants live. No, you still couldn't explain everything to the ants because it would still be beyond them to understand. What you could do, because you are now an ant as well as human, is speak at their level by releasing your own chemical that would lead them back to the backyard garden. The ants would have to follow your path only because they had faith in you and what you communicated to them they could not rely on their limited understanding.

No doubt the ant from the other anthill would try and stop you because he would fight to stay in control of the ants. That ant would release an attack chemical to the other ants whenever you and the ants that follow you are around. This would whip those other ants into a frenzy and cause them to try and kill you and the ants that follow you. The more you and your followers release the chemical of the path back to the garden the more the ant from the other anthill would try to have you killed, but more and more ants would still begin to follow you. Even some of the ants that were tricked into trying to kill you would become some of your faithful followers.

Alas that deceiving ant would think that if he killed you that the battle would be over. So it would only be a matter of time before you would be killed. Your followers though would continue to communicate to the other ants to follow the path you started, and every ant that followed that path would end up back in the garden with all the delicious fruit. The good news for you would be that even when you are killed by the unbelieving ants you would still be human. Only your ant body would die, and since your ant body was from your human body you could bring your ant body back, and because you would have power over your ant life you would have power over any ant life so that all those ants that were killed following your path you could bring back and place them in the garden.

And that old ant from the other anthill days would be numbered because once you were back to yourself you could have the exterminator deal with him whenever you wanted to. You wouldn't do it right away of course, because you would want as many of the deceived ants to come to follow your path as would come. After all you wouldn't want the deceived ants to die along with the ant from another anthill without having an opportunity to choose the right path and live.

That's it, the end of the mind trip. Now that we are done I just have two questions.

Number 1- Was this mind trip useless?
Number 2 - Can anyone help me understand why God had to become a man called Jesus?

Harry Potter VS the Ku Klux Klan

Some Christians are offended by Harry Potter. They say that because Harry practices witchcraft they cannot help but be offended. It would be something different, they say, if there was no such thing as real witchcraft but since there are real witches trying to war against humanity a witch, who is a hero, is offensive. I haven't had time to think about it much myself because I have been working on my own idea...

I am creating a character called Parry Hotter who is in training to be a grand wizard of the Ku Klux Klan. I know what you're thinking. You're thinking that this character would be offensive and people would not want to see him because being a Klansman can never be seen in a positive light.

Well, that's where you're wrong.

My young Klansman is not one of the bigoted bad Klansman, but my Klansman uses his skills for good. For instance; Parry does not burn crosses on the lawns of minority's, but he burns his crosses on the lawns of the bad bigoted Klansman. He puts on his white sheet and hood to terrorize these bad Klansman and drive them away to keep the minority's safe. When these bad Klansman refuse to leave and minorities remain in danger, then Parry has to go to the next level and he and his friends show up in the middle of the night at the bad Klansman's home and spirit them off and these bad Klansman will never be seen or heard of again.

We must keep in mind that Parry was forced to take this drastic action because the bad Klansman are so evil and bad that they left poor young Parry with no other choice.

You should also keep in mind that young Parry is really harmless, to the general public anyway, and is also so cute and innocent looking that no one could possibility be offended by him.

My character Parry Hotter should be no more offensive to the general public than Harry Potter is to Christians because when you are fighting evil, and very cute, whatever you are and whatever techniques you use can never be offensive. Right?...Right?

A Rabbi, A Priest and A Minister Walk Into A Bar...

A rabbi, a priest and a minister walk into a bar. The bartender looks up and says, "What's this, some kind of joke." Rim shot, cymbal crash!

Maybe it is some kind of joke, but should it be? The idea that a Godly leader has things, situations and places that he or she is above only serves to make such leadership irrelevant to the society that he or she should be serving. The perception that a bartender would be someone better to talk to about real life issues than a Godly leader is only possible when that leader feels above the people. Godly leadership disconnected from the people is the greatest of contradictions because it is also Godly leadership disconnected from God.

Jesus was in so called inappropriate settings and with inappropriate people so often he was called a drunkard and a friend of sinners. In fact you would be hard pressed to find where Jesus spoke a harsh word to any sinner except religious leaders. Jesus got involved in the lives of people in a positive way no matter what they had done or where they were. It is unfortunate but there are very many people who mistakenly feel that if Jesus met them he would never associate with them and he certainly would never do it in a bar.

Throughout history when Godly leadership is more devoted to their religious status within a society than to serving the people through God we find the most horrible crimes against people committed in the name of Christ. The seed for the horrors of the Spanish Inquisition where planted with the fertilizer of notions of superiority.

If we are honest we will agree that there have always been two groups that claimed to follow God. One in agreement with the world and living according to the principals of the world, and the other following God through his Word. Everything from Cain slaying his brother Abel to any present day religious violence and oppression is due to the worldly religion. The self-sacrifice, charity and unwillingness to see themselves above others are given to us from Godly relationship. There have been times in history where worldly religion has oppressed Godly relationship and there have been times when the lines have blurred between them. The important question for all of us is which group has given us our perception of God and therefore shaped how we live our lives?

If Jesus walked into a bar would the bartender think that it was the start of a joke or would he know that a bar would be one of Jesus's hangouts? Would the people in that bar know that Jesus was not there to look down on them but to hang out and offer them life?

The Atheist and the Train

I was telling my friend the atheist a story. As it turns out he didn't like my story and I don't know why. Maybe you can help me figure it out. The story I told my friend the atheist went like this.

Once upon a time there was a good politician who got a great idea at the train platform on his way to work. Every day he would talk to a homeless man that would come to the platform to beg for change. He would give the man money and after finding out that the man was dying from an incurable liver disease caused from drinking and drug use he felt he had to do something for the people in the city who were homeless and suffering. He would call it the Phoenix Initiative.

On this particular day the good politician was in the midst of a crisis. It had taken him five years to bring together, politicians, business men, educators, community leaders and public opinion to bring about the Phoenix Initiative. Tens of thousands of people would be helped and the entire city would be uplifted not just in the short term, but for generations. Many times his dream to help the city looked like it would die but the good politician was always able to save the day with his skill as a negotiator and his ability to make people believe that we can help one another and create a better world to live in.

This time it looked like even the skills of the good politician could not save the day. The good politician would not give up though. After a week and a half of phone calls and impromptu meetings it looked like he might yet pull it out. One last person had to be brought back on board so he changed into his suit on a Saturday afternoon with his phone to his ear and raced out of the door. He was not able to convince this last person over the phone but he knew if he met with them in person he could convince them to do the right thing. The good politician tied his tie as he ran the two blocks to the train which was the only way he could make it to this person before they left for Europe on business.

The good politician got to the train platform just in time. The train would be there in two or three minutes. He could already see it in the distance. Then a horrible revelation invaded his brain. He had rushed out so quickly that when he changed clothes he didn't change his wallet into his suit pocket. It was at home in his jeans. He had no way of paying for the train. He would miss the last meeting and the Phoenix Initiative would be dead. All he could think was that tens of thousands of people would suffer because he was absent minded.

Just then he saw the homeless man passed out in the gutter just off the platform and the sight of him sharpened the pain of his impending failure. Then a sudden idea gave him a sliver of hope. He shook the homeless man to ask him for his wine money. Not only did the homeless man say no, but he said he would be dead in a month or so and he didn't care what happened after he was gone. He also told the good politician to shut up and go away or he would cut him with his knife. The homeless man then rolled over in the gutter and passed out once more.

The good politician was undaunted. He took a large stone that was lying nearby and lifted it high above his head. The good politician paused for a second and then smashed the stone down on the homeless man's head. While the homeless man's legs where still twitching he took his wine money from his pocket and it was just enough to pay for his train. The good politician made his train and his meeting. The Phoenix Initiative was resurrected and tens of thousands of people where helped and the city was uplifted for generations to come.

The End.

My atheist Friend thought that it was a horrible story. Apparently he thought that the actions of the good politician were less than admirable to say the least.
Our conversation went something like this.

My atheist friend: It is wrong to murder someone for any reason, let alone train fare.

Confused me: But many more lives would be saved because of his actions.

My atheist Friend: You can't arbitrarily take a human life just because you think it serves the greater good.

Confused me: Why not, if there is no God.

My atheist friend- Don't be ridiculous. If we do not hold to a human standard of goodness we are doomed. We don't need a creator God to believe that.

Confused me-: This is exactly my point. As humans we must choose for the greater good. If you believe life is an accidental combination of inert materials from a primordial soup, then the only value it has is what we assign to it. The homeless man was not ever going to contribute to the greater good. The homeless man had been chosen by evolution to perish because of his illness. There was no way to assign value to his life outside of every life being sacred because it is a gift from God. So if there is no God, then the greater good was for him to die and for thousands of others to be helped.

My atheist friend: You are confused and obviously unable to understand the most basic tenants of a secular humanistic philosophy as it pertains to the good of mankind.

Confused me: That's strange, your last statement sounded like what has been said by many people throughout history that destroyed human life for what they perceived as the greater good. Are you sure you don't like my story?

My atheist friend then stormed off. He still couldn't explain to me why he didn't like my story but I think I may have figured it out. I think it is simply this, what we sometimes believe in theory is very different when we see it in practice. What is scary to me is that we don't usually discover this until it is too late.

Lesson

That woman Jezebel who calls herself a prophetess was violently attacking the preachers of God. She attacked God's preachers by telling the people that the preachers knew not the love of their God. She then told God's people that because their God loved them he did not require a holy lifestyle. Her plan is always to seduce the people teaching them all to worship their flesh.

She rose up false preachers to support all her teaching and lead most away from the Word of their God. The false teachers taught that sin would not hurt them and to sin in their flesh was acceptable to God. So God sent to them a drought and a famine to warn all his people of serving their flesh. The people ignored God's sovereign warning for the flesh has its pleasure and people will serve it though painful and violent and wicked it is. They did not believe that their God was yet willing to search hearts and minds and then judge their flesh. The Word to them had become without meaning since Jezebel taught that God could be mocked.

Then God sent a preacher to speak to the people and teach them a lesson of the power of His Word. The preacher stood at the top of Mount Carmel and said, "Serve God's Word or trust in your flesh!" The people stood tall and silent before him for God was not feared, they feared only flesh.

The preacher then challenged all the false preachers to call on the flesh to heal and deliver. The false preachers preached from morning to evening but nothing miraculous happened for them. The preacher then preached the Word of his Father and the Father moved with fire and power and the people were changed and trusted God's Word and moved the false preachers away from their lives. The father then sent them rain and provision and

the people were healed and the people were delivered
and the people rejoiced in the love of their God.

Such is the preacher's battle with the flesh.

Prodigals

It came to pass that the men from man came before the prophet seeking to question him and justify themselves before him.

And so it was that the first man from man came forward and said: "I am moral and most religious. Therefore I ask you this prophet; why do you say that God loves the poor in spirit when we all know that unless someone lives as well as we do they will not see heaven?"
The prophet then said: "Man from man I have something to say to you." and the man from man said, "Say on!" The prophet then said, "The words of your own mouth testify against you for God has not called us to morality but to Holiness. Holiness is God's standard for life for those who love him. This standard grows out of the relationship he has with his people. Morality is humanity's ever changing standard to justify itself before God and the world around us.

God has also not called us to religion but to salvation. Religion is humanity's attempt to reach God through its own ability but salvation is God's specific plan to reconcile lost humanity to him. But as for your question; the poor in spirit know that they are in need and therefore are rich but those who consider themselves rich in spirit are self-sufficient and therefore poor. Now go find the meaning of these words; 'I desire mercy and not sacrifice."

Then the man from man fell back in the dust with much weeping and gnashing of teeth.

The next man from man came forward and said: "I am Marx, and I say that you make claims that God makes us all free but in reality humanity has been made slaves, chained in a capitalistic environment where they are alienated and estranged from themselves and others. All of your claims that God improves our lives are simply lies to lull us into complacency so that we can be more easily controlled. Your teachings are nothing more than the opiate of the masses."

And the prophet answered him and said: "You foolish blind guide! You profess to see clearly but it is your own blind arrogance that is destroying you. Yours is the sin committed at the tower of Babel, yours is the hardness of heart that Judas and many others have shown God. Like Babel you are trying to elevate your life without God. Like Judas you only see the things outside of the human heart, humanity's carnal needs and environment. You are blind to what God offers though he stands before you day after day. You fail to see that it is not humanity's environment or need that brings about evil, but it is the condition of sin. You can change every person's environment into what you consider the perfect utopia but wickedness will still prevail until you can free us all from the fallen condition of sin. Every society from the very beginning contained violence and degradation. Even so called innocent humans living in remote rain forest away from a capitalistic system, and with relatively plentiful resources all around them commit murder, steal, and lie. You can't see that God has destroyed the power of sin and called men to a quality life. In this present world, the freedom that God gives is the only utopia possible with perfection attained in the world to come.

As for the rest of your claims; you have seen people come in God's name claiming to be of God. These are ravenous wolves, clouds without rain, which walk in a form of Godliness, but deny the power thereof. They have deceived some and murdered others. These are what you call the opiate of the masses. You fail to see the most obvious opiate which is sin and the blindness that sin brings. God's words are true no matter how many liars who pretend to be of God enter the world. God is your only way to true freedom, therefore repent or your destruction in the coming tribulation is sure."

The second man from man fell back in the dust with much weeping and gnashing of teeth.

Then the next man from man came forward and said,: "I am a spiritual being reaching for a higher spiritual plane and I see that your teaching doesn't include all that it should. How can your followers reach a higher spiritual plane when they eat meat and break many other laws written in their own bodies?"

The Prophet said: "You have been blinded by the basic principles of this world. You can't see that it is not what goes in a person's mouth but what comes out that defiles them. You live by instinct always learning but never able to accept the truth. You ,like the Pharisees of old, think, that you can be justified spiritually by your own works. This is impossible. It is by God's grace through faith only that you can reach a higher spiritual plane. This is God's gift to you.

Yours is a doctrine of the physical not the spiritual. Even if you followed the laws of your body in the strictest sense your spiritual righteousness would be like filthy rags. When you stay in bed one half second longer than God intended a human to stay in bed you are a sluggard. If you eat one half teaspoonful more food than God intended a human to eat, you are a glutton. You fail to see that sin is your condition not things that you choose to do. You can never trust your instincts and intuition to lead you to a higher spiritual plane for all of humanity's nature was warped at Eden.

I tell you the truth; when you follow all of your natural laws you will still only live three score and ten years or four score if you have the strength then you will die. Your physical laws have no power over death. God has given us the way and the truth and the life, no one comes to God the father but by his son Jesus who is Christ. Your only hope to escape death and move to a higher spiritual plane is through the simple plan of salvation, which is justification through Jesus Christ, yet you do not believe in him so you stand condemned already. Go now and understand the meaning of this saying; 'You must be born again."

And the man from man fell back in the dust with much weeping and gnashing of teeth.

The next man from man came forward and said: "I am the atheist. I believe that there can't be a God who would allow all this pain and suffering in the world and furthermore, a loving God would not punish people with an eternal hell for making mistakes in this meaningless life." The prophet then said; "It is yours to believe: If you do not believe today you will have no choice but to believe it on that day.

As for your statement; when humanity surrendered its authority to the enemy through Adam in Eden the enemy became the prince of this world in our stead and sin resulted. All of creation is warped and cursed by sin and the resulting pain and death comes from the enemy of all creation. Through our own authority, our enemy deceives us into twisting and warping the system of the world. The pain and suffering you speak of is all of us acting on the deceptive direction given. No wickedness can exist without the authority of a participating human being. It is through Christ that we can again take up our God given authority and destroy the wickedness that we find and bring what is good and loving into the world.

As for sending people to hell for making mistakes, God will send no one to hell. Hell was not prepared for the souls of men but for the enemy and his fallen angels. The only humans that will go to hell are those who remain submitted to the enemy's authority and therefore part of his rebellion against God. A human's life is only meaningless when lived for itself apart from God. The meaning of life is found in this saying; "God so loved the world that he gave his only begotten Son and anyone who believes in him shall not perish but have everlasting life." Anyone who does not accept this saying is choosing hell on his own.

A man who walks off a cliff cannot accuse the bridge for being ignored. Jesus is the bridge over the chasm of sin and death and I stand now inviting you to cross. All who show the wisdom of crossing the bridge will be saved but all who follow the foolishness of walking off the cliff will fall into everlasting destruction."

The man from man fell back into the dust with much trembling.

Then the next man from man came forward and said: "I am living for free love. How can you condemn love of any kind? Any and all type of love is still love. How can you speak against me if God created me this way? Do you realize when you speak against me you are speaking against God who made me."

Then the prophet said: "You are deceived and taken captive to do evil against your own self. Yours is the most common reason for sin in the human heart for you say if I justify something in my own mind then it is acceptable to God. Do you not see that there is an eternal law that existed before the foundation of the world, and that your own reasons and justifications are of no consequence?

You speak of love but yours is not love but warped emotions. The enemy has caused a deep seated hurt in your soul and uses this hurt to twist your emotions into expressing this lifestyle. From infancy the enemy has been hurting you and preparing you for this deception. Christ has died for you and loves you and has his hand extended to you to heal your emotions. This is true love. God is love so you cannot love anyone else outside of the law and love of God. You cannot express love through sin but through sin you will only express powerful twisted emotion.

You reject God's love and choose your emotions to justify your lifestyle. True love includes but is more than emotions. Emotions alone cannot lead you to love. Love flows through a relationship with God into us then out from us to the world around us. This is the only free love that exists for all other love is based on selfish emotion and has a cost attached. Understand there is no free love but God. God is free love.

You also claim that you are without guilt for you were created this way. The enemy works hurt and pain even in the womb, so from the beginning he has planted such deceptions in your heart. This deception started from your earliest memories and is associated with pain and rejection but you do not seek to be delivered from this deception or made whole, indeed you are seeking justification to continue in your wickedness. Your inclusion in the coming destruction is sure."

The man from man fell back into the dust with much weeping and gnashing of teeth.

The next man from man came forward and said: "I am a great Christian leader and I have seen that your views don't always agree with mine. What is the meaning of this?"

The prophet said: "The meaning of this is simple. You follow the doctrines of men. You draw nigh onto God with your mouth but your heart is far from him. God says the greatest of these is love but you won't give the poor a place among you in your pews, but only condescending charity and sometimes not even that. You look down on those who have been arrested and thrown in prison or are the rejected of our society. God says love not the world but you live according to every principal of the world. God says be Holy for I am Holy but you practice all types of wickedness. You don't study God's Word or even know it but the traditions of your own denomination you take as truth. He who is not for Christ is against Christ he who does not gather with Christ scatters. Repent or you will be like the unwise virgins who had no oil and were left out in the darkness where there was weeping and gnashing of teeth."

The man from man fell back into the dust with much weeping and sorrow.

Then the last man from man came forward and said: "I am new age and I see that there are many truths. You shouldn't be so closed minded. Many sincere people are seeking help from spirit guides and others in the spirit world."

The prophet said to him: "Yes people are receiving from the spirit world but it is not help. They are receiving lies, deceptions and a gateway to eternal destruction as are you.

You say in your heart that everything that comes from the spirit world that feels helpful is good. You fail to recognize that there are powers, principalities and spiritual wickedness in high places who can transform themselves into angels of light. Even the enemy himself can appear to be an angel of light. These spirit deceivers give you sugar coated subtle deceptions and you receive them to your bosom.

Don't you know that in ancient Egypt the powers of darkness replicated many of the acts that God did through Moses? This is the spiritual reality you are receiving. You call yourself 'New Age' but in reality yours is wickedness of old. Indeed the same lie that was told in Eden has been told to you by your spirit guides. The enemy told Eve that she would be like God and he tells you today that you are all God. Don't you know that from the beginning God forbade any spiritualist to be among his people? If you continue down this path you will share the drink of the cup of God's wrath with the rest of the lost."

The man from man fell back with much weeping and gnashing of teeth.

Then the Lord himself looked out from heaven to see all that goes on in the earth and the Lord said: "All creation is struggling with the berth pains of that great day and I perceive that the harvest is plentiful but the workers are few. Who can I send to help with the harvest?"

Then the men from man came forward trembling with head bowed and while they were still afar off they stopped and said: "Sovereign Lord, we now know you to be the only wise God and savior of the world. We know we are not worthy to come into your presence but we plead with you to count not our sin against others like us. Though we are destined to be lost send us to warn the world so they will not share in our destruction."

Then the Lord's heart was touched and his love was manifested to the men from man and he said to them: "Men of God rise out of the dust. Come now and receive the white robes that were prepared for you before the foundation of the world."

Then the men from man that had been transformed into the men of God received their white robes, laying their former clothes aside and went forward throughout the earth proclaiming the good news of forgiveness for humanity and God's loving way to eternal life. And when the full measure of time had passed, they each went to their reward of eternal life and joy unspeakable and there they remained always along with all those who humble themselves before the knowledge of the Lord.

Parable

There was once a kingdom who sometimes forgot what they were born to do. They forgot too often and remembered too slowly.

One day their forgetfulness was seen in the fear of a giant who made his stand in the middle of a valley. This giant stood daily in the middle of the valley for the shadow of valleys are where giants wax strong, and defied the courage of the forgetful kingdom. The kingdom shrank back from the defying giant for they feared to try and slay such as he and they feared to walk through the valley of shadow.

There was once a young poet who was charged by his father to take courage alone in faraway valleys. He was charged by his father to kill lion and bear with only such tools as a poet might have. So he learned to trust his father's command when he was alone and no one else saw.

One day this poet was sent by his father to the valley of Elah to strengthen his brothers and he saw the giant yet defying the kingdom and his anger was kindled and he said aloud; "Who is this giant to defy this kingdom, a kingdom well able to slay such as he? For my father I killed both lion and bear this giant will be like one of these!"

He went forth with the tools to kill lion and bear, only such tools as a poet might have. He did not fear the valley of shadow, for he had walked through valleys before, and he slew the giant like the lion and bear with the unimpressive tools of his father's command.

The forgetful kingdom saw this and then they remembered that they were well able to slay such as he and they feared no longer the valley off shadow and in their new courage they charged boldly forward and won a great victory for then they remembered that this is what they were born to do.

Such is the Father's call of a Christian poet.

Be the message!

52977731R00070

Made in the USA
Charleston, SC
27 February 2016